Oxford
Reading
Tree

FACT
FINDERS

Families

Getting re **d**

Roderick Hunt

Oxford University Press

Adam and Yasmin are Muslims.

This book is about their family.

They are getting ready for Eid-ul-Fitr.

Contents

Page

▶ Learning about Muslims.........4

▶ Ramadan daytime...................6

▶ Ramadan evenings 8

▶ Grandmother's visit...............10

▶ Getting ready for Eid 12

▶ Eid-ul-Fitr 14

▶ Index 16

Learning about Muslims

Grandfather has come to school.
He has come to tell the children
about Ramadan and Eid-ul-Fitr.
Ramadan comes before Eid.

Muslims praying.

A Koran

Grandfather shows the children a Koran.

The Koran is the Muslim holy book.

It teaches about Allah.

Allah is the Muslim name for God.

Ramadan daytime

Ramadan is a special time for Muslims.

They do not eat or drink during the day.

This is called fasting.

Little children do not fast at Ramadan.

Yasmin is old enough to fast for
one day.
The grown-ups fast for a month.

Ramadan evenings

When it gets dark, Yasmin can eat.
The grown-ups are pleased with Yasmin.
Fasting for a day was hard for her.

Yasmin understands why Muslims fast.
Fasting shows them what it is
like to be poor and hungry.
At Ramadan, Muslims give to the poor.

Grandmother's visit

Ramadan will soon be over.

Then it will be Eid-ul-Fitr.

Eid is a happy time for Muslims.

Families like to be together at Eid, so
Grandmother has come to stay.
She has come from Pakistan.

Getting ready for Eid

It is the end of Ramadan.

Grandmother is painting Yasmin's hands.

The painting is called mendhi.

Muslim women paint their hands for Eid.

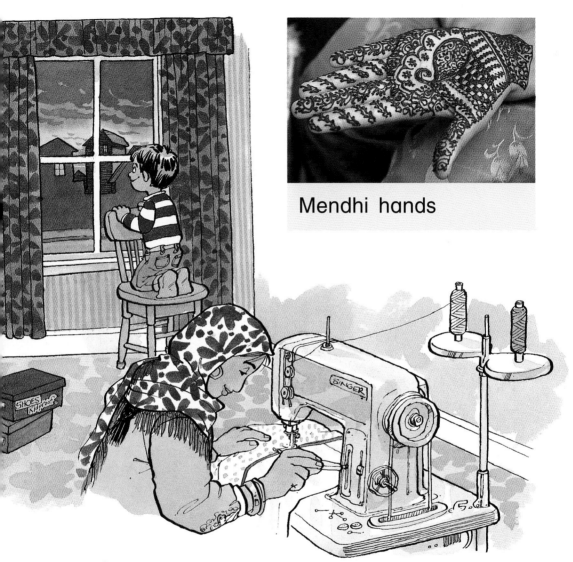

Mendhi hands

Mum makes new clothes for everyone.
Adam is looking for the moon.
Eid will begin when the moon
comes out.

Eid-ul-Fitr

Eid-ul-Fitr has begun.
Everyone wears their new clothes.
Now, it is time to give presents and
wish everyone a happy Eid.

Soon, it will be time to eat.

First, everyone will say a prayer.

They will thank Allah for good things.

Index

Allah 5, 15

Eid-ul-Fitr 4, 10–11, 12–13, 14–15

fasting 6–7, 8–9

Koran 5

mendhi hands 12

new moon 13

Ramadan 4, 6–7, 8–9, 10, 12

Oxford University Press, Great Clarendon Street, Oxford OX2 6DP

© Oxford University Press
All rights reserved

First published by Oxford University Press 1994
Reprinted 1995, 1998 (twice)

ISBN 0 19 916640 4
Available in packs
Families pack (one of each title)
ISBN 0 19 916642 0
Families class pack (six of each title)
ISBN 0 19 916643 9

Teacher's Guide ISBN 0 19 916670 6

Acknowledgements

Photographs: Peter Saunders

Illustrated by: David Parkins

Cover illustration: David Parkins

Printed and bound in Hong Kong